The Thirteen Colonies

Reader

Core Knowledge®

ISBN: 978-1-68380-181-8

The Thirteen Colonies

Table of Contents

Plan for the City of Philadelphia

Baire Mount

Scool Kill River

River Delaware

The Thirteen Colonies
Reader
Core Knowledge History and Geography™

Chapter 1
The English Colonies

Thirteen in All The United States began as a group of thirteen English colonies. These thirteen colonies did not begin all at once. Explorers and **traders** came first. Then slowly, over time, the colonies were created. The first colony was founded in Virginia in 1607, and the last of the thirteen colonies was founded in Georgia in 1732.

The Big Question

Why did people come to settle in the English colonies?

Vocabulary

trader, n. a person who buys and sells things

The first European settlers came here from England. They brought with them everything they owned. When the settlers arrived, they had no family to greet them. Sometimes the Native Americans who already lived in North America welcomed the settlers. Other times, however, the Native Americans were not happy to see newcomers settling on their land.

There were no houses to live in, so many of the first settlers lived in tents. Some even lived in caves to survive. Their living conditions were harsh, especially during the winter. Many died of hunger, cold, and disease.

The first English settlers hoped to find a new life in the colonies.

Even though life in the early colonies could be hard, most settlers did not return to England. They started a new life in a new place instead.

Why They Came

Early settlers had different reasons for coming to America. Some people came because they had been very poor in their homeland. In England and other countries, there were often not enough jobs or land. The new colonies needed workers, and as far as the settlers were concerned, there was enough land for everyone who wanted to stay. People who settle in a new place on behalf of another country are called colonists. The settlers were, in fact, colonists.

Some colonists came because they thought they could get rich in America. Some hoped to find gold and silver. Others hoped that farming would make them wealthy. Some were people who had broken the law in England and, as part of their punishment, they were sent to the colonies in North America.

Some people hoped to become very rich in this new land.

Even though it was not easy to live in the colonies, many people believed they would have a better life.

Colonists came for religious reasons, too. In England, not everyone could practice their religion in the way that they wanted. Some people came to America because they wanted to worship in their own way. For these colonists, living in a land where they could have religious freedom was important.

Not everyone who crossed the Atlantic Ocean found opportunity and freedom. As the colonies developed and grew larger, some people from Africa were forced to settle in America. They did not choose to settle here. Instead, they were kidnapped from their homes and brought across the ocean to be enslaved workers.

The New England Colonies

The map shows that the colonies were divided into three groups, or **regions**.

The New England Colonies made up the northern region. They included Massachusetts, New Hampshire,

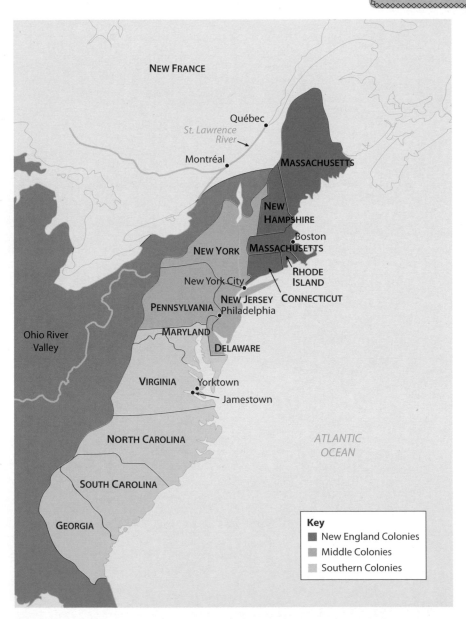

The English colonies were divided into three regions.

Connecticut, and Rhode Island. Originally, there was another colony In New England called Plymouth, which you will read about later. Plymouth eventually became part of Massachusetts.

In New England, the winters were long and cold. The soil was rocky. The short growing season and poor soil made it difficult for the colonists to grow **crops** there.

Usually, New England colonists grew only enough vegetables and grains to feed their own families. They were unable to grow extra food to sell to others.

Just like today, the New England region had a long coastline with many natural **harbors**. Fish were plentiful in the rivers and in the coastal waters.

When the colonists first arrived, they found many forests in the region. The colonists cut down trees for **timber**. They used the timber to build ships, houses, and other buildings. Timber was also used for firewood.

As the colonies grew, trading ships sailed in and out of the busy New England harbors. The ships carried timber to the West Indies, the Caribbean, and Europe.

> ## Vocabulary
>
> **crop,** n. a plant that is grown in large quantities for food or other use
>
> **harbor,** n. a part of a body of water that is next to land and provides a safe place for ships to anchor
>
> **timber,** n. wood that is cut from trees and used for building; lumber

The Middle Colonies

The colonies in the middle region were called the Middle Colonies. They were New York, New Jersey, Pennsylvania, and Delaware.

Because of the climate and soil, wheat grew well in the Middle Colonies.

Winters in the Middle Colonies were not as long and cold as the winters in New England. Warm, rainy summers and fertile soil made growing crops much easier in this region. Colonists in the Middle Colonies could grow enough food to feed themselves and still have crops left over to sell. The Middle Colonies also had a coastline for fishing and ports for ships.

The Southern Colonies

The Southern Colonies were made up of Maryland, Virginia, North Carolina, South Carolina, and Georgia.

The Southern Colonies were perfect for farming. They had mild winters and fertile soil. Crops grew so well that some colonists built large farms called plantations. Many plantations grew large amounts of a single crop that was then sold to make a profit.

Port Cities

As more people from England and other European countries came to America, the colonists built towns that often grew into cities. Have you heard of Boston, New York, Philadelphia, and Charleston? These cities became known as port cities. This is because they were built along waterways or on harbors on the coast. The colonists used waterways for transportation.

Centers of Trade

Port cities became centers for trade, too. They also became places where news and information were shared. Ships traveling between the port cities kept the colonies connected with each other and with the rest of the world.

New ideas spread from the port cities throughout the colonies. One of the ideas that developed over time was that the colonists could govern themselves. When you learn about the American Revolution, you will read about how the colonists fought to create an independent nation.

Chapter 2
Starting the Virginia Colony

An Ocean Apart It was September in the year 1607, and Hannah was not happy at all. She was trying to read a new book, but it was too difficult for her.

The Big Question
....
What challenges did the colonists in Jamestown face?

If Thomas were home, here in London, he would have helped her. But Thomas had gone away last year, when she was seven, to a place called Virginia. Hannah often thought about Thomas. Sometimes she worried about him because he had set off on a dangerous voyage across the giant ocean.

Thomas was Hannah's uncle, her father's younger brother. But he had always lived with her family in London, and Hannah thought of him as her big brother. Thomas was eighteen years old, and Hannah was eight. She missed Thomas.

In 1607, ships carried the first English settlers—such as Hannah's Uncle Thomas—to North America.

Letter from Jamestown

"Hannah, Hannah, come quickly! We have a letter from Thomas!" Mother was very excited.

Hannah raced into the parlor. She laughed and jumped up and down before falling into a chair. "What does Thomas say? Oh, read it, please, Mother. Read it to me, please!"

Hannah's mother unfolded the letter. She laughed. She looked so happy. She had worried about Thomas, too. "His letter is dated June 1607. That was more than three months ago! Virginia certainly is far away," Hannah's mother said.

Thomas began his letter, "To my family:

"Six months ago our three ships, the *Discovery*, the *Godspeed*, and the *Susan Constant*, sailed from England. We men of the Virginia Company of London were eager to sail. We thought the adventure in Virginia would make us rich.

"We were at sea four long months before we saw land again. During those months, we grew very tired of sailing—and of each other.

"One man argued with Mr. Edward Wingfield, a very important man aboard the ship. The poor fellow was then locked in chains for the rest of the voyage. I became friends with that man, and he has proved to be a most unusual fellow.

"We finally reached the Chesapeake Bay in April. That's when I saw Virginia for the first time. It is a beautiful land, with great forests and green fields. The water in the bay is clear and deep and filled with fish.

"We were all so happy to see land stretching out before us."

Instructions from London

"We put ashore at a point we called Cape Henry, named for the king's oldest son. Shortly afterward, Captain Newport of the *Susan Constant* brought out a sea chest. Instructions from the Virginia Company had been locked in there since we left England.

"We were to follow the instructions. First, we were to sail up a deep river and find a place for a settlement. Then we were to build a fort to protect us from attack.

"The instructions included the names of seven men who were to make rules for the colony. They would be called the **council**. Six of those names were no surprise to us at all, for they were important **gentlemen** or ship captains.

"But one name was a great surprise to everyone—John Smith. John Smith was not a rich gentleman. He was the man who had been locked in chains below **deck**, my new friend.

Vocabulary

gentleman, n. a man with high position in society; not a laborer

deck, n. the floor of a ship that people walk on

"The six gentlemen who were named to the council would not accept John Smith as an equal. They would not let him on the council, but they did take off his chains.

Jamestown

"We followed the Virginia Company's instructions. We sailed up a clear, deep river, which we named the James River after the king. About sixty miles upriver, we came upon a place that all the gentlemen thought would be just right for our settlement. This place would be safe and unnoticed by our enemy, the Spanish. We named the place Jamestown, once again in honor of King James.

The passengers were happy to leave their ships after such a long voyage.

"We were all very happy to get off the ships and onto land. But trouble began almost at once.

"Our first task was to build a fort to protect us from Native Americans and the Spanish. Most of us had never built anything before. Many of the gentlemen had never worked a day in their lives, and they did not want to work now. What they really wanted was for someone else to do the work while they looked for gold.

"John Smith knew a lot about building. He showed me how to chop down trees and carve them into thick posts.

"He also showed me how to bury the lower part of the posts into the ground close together so that they could stand up straight. These posts became a strong wall called the **palisade** that protected the fort.

Finding Food

"John Smith took me to the river each day to fish. Sometimes the other gentlemen joined us, but they rarely caught anything. Smith almost always caught fish for us to eat. I watched him carefully and did what he did. Soon I was able to catch fish, too.

"Smith also taught me how to find other foods. I learned where to look for berries and nuts. Native Americans watched us as we worked.

"After a few weeks of hard work, the fort was partly finished. But then the council decided to send Captain Newport and John Smith to explore farther up the James River. I wanted to go, too. I wanted to see more of the land.

"John Smith did not want to explore the James River. He did not want anyone else to explore it, either. He thought we should finish the fort first.

"Many of the gentlemen were angry because they had not found any gold. They did very little except eat, sleep, and argue.

"Smith became angry. He said it was very important to prepare for the coming winter. The council did not listen to Smith. They ordered us to explore the river instead.

Trouble at the Fort

"We did as we were told and left to explore the river. We traveled up the river for several days. Eventually, we came to a place where the water ran over huge rocks that could destroy our boat. We had to return to Jamestown.

"When we got back, we heard bad news. While we were gone, there had been conflict between the men left behind and Native Americans. Two of our men were killed. Ten more were wounded. The fort had also been damaged.

"John Smith had been right, and the council had been wrong. Now the council was ready to listen to John Smith. He told the men to get to work and rebuild the fort.

"I am happy to say that we finished the fort a few days ago. Captain Smith, as everyone calls him now, took his seat on the council.

"The ship that will carry our letters home to England is about to sail. If the ship does not sink on the way and you get this letter, please write back to me. I will write again when the next ship sails.

Your loving Thomas."

John Smith knew that it was important to prepare for the cold winter months.

Chapter 3
Captain John Smith

News from Jamestown Hannah and her mother wrote a letter back to Thomas. They told him that they missed him very much and asked him to write again as soon as he could.

The Big Question

How did John Smith make sure that everyone worked?

Months later, in the spring of 1608, Thomas's next letter arrived. Captain Newport brought the letter when he returned from Jamestown.

"To my family," Thomas's letter began. "There have been many changes in our life here in Jamestown. In many ways, life has been hard, but we are working to keep our tiny colony alive. We owe our lives to John Smith. Without him, none of us would be alive today.

"When John Smith took his seat on the council, we were running low on food. He knew that it was too late in the year to plant crops. He also knew that the Native Americans who we now knew as the Powhatan (/pow*at*an/) had corn and other food. John Smith began visiting their villages. I often went with him. He began to learn their language and their way of life.

John Smith taught people in Jamestown how to survive.

"We began to trade. We gave the Powhatan blankets, axes, and other things from England. In exchange, they gave us corn and fresh meat. Their food kept everyone from starving. We can all thank Captain Smith—and the Powhatan—for saving our colony."

Three Years Later

It was a long time before Hannah and her mother received another letter from Thomas. Finally, in 1611, news from Thomas arrived.

"Please forgive me for waiting so long to write. I wanted to send you good news about Jamestown, but it was a long time before things got better.

"In fact, life in the colony became even harder than at the beginning, and many men died. The people living in Jamestown could not learn to work together. The council could not make life better for the colony.

A New Rule

"Then the council chose John Smith to be the leader of the colony. Smith made a new rule. Those who did not work could not eat. Some of the gentlemen complained, but Smith stayed firm. He would not change the rule.

"After Captain Smith's new rule, more work got done. The fort was made larger, and more houses were built. We dug a **well** so we could have cleaner water to drink.

> **Vocabulary**
>
> **well,** n. a hole dug deep into the ground to get water

New houses were built within the fort.

We cleared fields, planted crops, and caught fish. We traded more with the Native Americans. Captain Smith also taught us to use weapons to defend the fort.

"Captain Newport will sail back to England with a cargo of timber and boards cut from the forest in Jamestown by English gentlemen.

Your loving Thomas."

Chapter 4
Changing Times in Jamestown

Working Together Many things went well when John Smith was the leader of Jamestown. The settlement grew to nearly five hundred people. The colonists all worked because John Smith had made a rule that those who did not work could not eat.

The Big Question

What events led to the Starving Time?

The colonists grew crops. They raised chickens, goats, and horses. They also kept pigs outside the fort in a place called Hog Island.

In the forests around Jamestown, there were many animals for the colonists to hunt. They could catch fish and oysters in the rivers and the Chesapeake Bay. They could gather the fruits, berries, and nuts that grew wild in the Jamestown area.

John Smith traded for food with the Powhatan. They were willing to trade with him because he worked hard to earn their respect. He was fair and honest. He always kept his word.

John Smith was a fair and honest leader.

New Problems

Then one night a terrible thing happened. Captain Smith was very badly hurt in a **gunpowder** explosion. He had to return to England for medical help to heal his wounds.

When Captain Smith left, the colonists had a good supply of food in their storehouses. They had enough for more than two months. They also had a clean water supply, warm houses, and a strong fort.

Many of the colonists were happy to see John Smith go back to England. They were tired of working so hard. But after he left, the colonists were missing something important—a good leader.

A gunpowder explosion in Jamestown injured Captain Smith.

The new leader was not as strong as Captain Smith had been. He did not make the colonists work hard to survive.

A group of colonists went to trade with the Powhatan, but they tried to cheat the Native Americans. A fight broke out, and the colonists were killed.

Now the Powhatan were angry, and they would not trade for food. The colonists' food supply continued to grow smaller.

Outnumbered, the colonists were trapped inside the walls of the Jamestown fort. The colonists could not go out to hunt or fish. They also needed firewood for the coming winter. The people of Jamestown began knocking down the houses they had worked so hard to build.

The Starving Time

The colonists grew hungry. Before long, they had eaten everything in the storehouses. Then they ate the chickens, the goats, and even the horses. After the large animals were gone, the colonists ate the dogs and then the cats. Then they ate the rats and finally the mice. They were so hungry that they even ate their boots and shoes.

Many of the colonists died from hunger, disease, and freezing temperatures. By the spring of 1610, only sixty people were still alive. The colonists had a special name for the winter of 1609 and the spring of 1610. They called it the Starving Time.

Many people died from the cold and hunger during the Starving Time.

A New Leader

The colonists decided to leave Jamestown, but they did not get far. As they sailed down the James River, they saw sails in the distance.

The sails belonged to two English ships on their way to Jamestown. The ships carried a new **governor**, more new colonists, and lots of supplies. The colony was saved!

The new governor was a strong leader. He warned the colonists that they would be punished if they did not work hard. He ordered everyone to clean up and rebuild the settlement.

A New Start

Finally the Starving Time was over. The colonists began to clear the land around the fort. They built small farmhouses. The English colonists in Virginia had survived their worst struggles. Slowly life in Jamestown began to get better. The Powhatan and the colonists began to trade again. But neither side fully trusted the other anymore.

Chapter 5
Virginia Succeeds

The Native American Princess

Captain John Smith had become friends with Chief Powhatan of the Powhatan tribe. The chief had a daughter whom he loved very much.

The Big Question

How did the arrival of John Rolfe affect the Virginia colony?

Chief Powhatan gave her the pet name Pocahontas (/poh*kuh*hon*tas/), which means the playful one. Pocahontas visited the Jamestown colony many times. She taught John Smith some Powhatan words. She brought food to the colonists and tried to make peace with them.

Pocahontas was about fourteen years old when John Smith was injured by the gunpowder explosion and had to leave Jamestown.

Pocahontas hoped to make peace with the English settlers.

Saved by a Shipwreck

At about the same time John Smith was sailing back to England, another Englishman, named John Rolfe, was on his way to Virginia. There were two interesting things about John Rolfe. First, he was a very, very lucky man. Second, like many people of his time, he really liked to smoke his pipe.

In 1609, several ships left England bound for Jamestown. One ship was called the *Sea Venture* and another was called the *Catch*. John Rolfe sailed aboard the *Sea Venture*.

Things did not go very well. The ships were caught in a storm. The *Catch* and all of its passengers sank to the bottom of the ocean. The *Sea Venture* was wrecked on an island seven hundred miles from Jamestown. It could not be repaired. The only way for

A bad storm threatened the ships. The *Catch* sank to the bottom of the ocean.

everyone to get to Jamestown was to make two smaller ships from the remaining pieces of the *Sea Venture*.

It took a long time to build the two ships. By the time the ships finally reached Jamestown, they were almost a year late.

Because of the shipwreck, Rolfe and the men with him were not in Jamestown during the Starving Time. Many of the people in Jamestown during that awful time had died.

Soon after Rolfe reached Jamestown, he ran out of **tobacco** for his pipe. He had been smoking tobacco that the Spanish had brought to Europe from the Americas. Now Rolfe tried the tobacco that the Native Americans in Virginia grew. He did not like it at all.

> **Vocabulary**
>
> **tobacco,** n. a plant whose leaves are used for chewing or smoking
>
> **cash crop,** n. a crop that is grown to be sold

John Rolfe left Jamestown and moved farther up the James River. There, he started a farm near the new village of Henrico (/hen*rye*koh/).

Growing Tobacco

Rolfe decided to buy seeds of the tobacco that grew in South America and seeds of the tobacco that grew in the West Indies. He tested the different kinds of tobacco plants to find one that would grow well in Virginia. Soon Rolfe was growing excellent tobacco and shipping it back to England.

People in England liked John Rolfe's Virginia tobacco, too. It quickly became Virginia's **cash crop**.

Everywhere in the colony, people started planting tobacco—even in the streets and in graveyards. Soon the colony was shipping thousands of pounds of Virginia tobacco to England.

In 1619, the people of Jamestown established the House of Burgesses. This was the first example of **self-government** in the colonies. Also, colonists were now able to own land and keep the money earned from the tobacco they sold. The ability for people to make money from tobacco increased the need for land and for workers.

Smoking became very popular in England. Few English people understood how unhealthy it was. King James was one of the

Growing tobacco made Virginia a rich colony.

few people in England who decided that smoking was bad. He wrote a book called *A Counterblast to Tobacco* that warned against smoking the "stinking weed." Smoking, he said, was "loathsome [disgusting] to the eye, hateful to the nose, harmful to the brain," and also "dangerous to the lungs." But no one paid attention.

More Adventures for Pocahontas

Meanwhile, Pocahontas went to visit some friends in a nearby village. While she was there, an English sea captain kidnapped her. He took her up the river to the village of Henrico.

When Pocahontas got to Henrico, the women there gave her English clothes to wear. They taught her to speak English and to read the Bible. Pocahontas took the name Rebecca.

John Rolfe met Pocahontas in Henrico. The Native American princess fell in love with him. Her father, Chief Powhatan, said they could get married. Everyone was happy for Pocahontas and John Rolfe. Their marriage meant that the Powhatan and the colonists lived in peace for several years.

A year after Pocahontas and John Rolfe were married, their son Thomas was born. They took the baby to England to visit John Rolfe's family.

While Pocahontas was in England, everyone treated her like a queen. They called her Lady Rebecca. She made many new friends there, including King James. She also had a happy meeting with her old friend Captain John Smith.

The Native American princess met the king of England.

Pocahontas was about to leave England to go home when she caught a terrible **disease** and died. She was only twenty-two years old. She was buried in England.

The same year that Pocahontas died, the Virginia colony shipped twenty thousand pounds of tobacco to England. The gentlemen of Virginia intended to get rich growing tobacco. To do this, they cleared new land for large farms called plantations. Because they owned plantations, they came to be known as "planters." At first, planters, like John Rolfe, thought that growing tobacco would make them as rich as if they had found gold.

John Rolfe was a very lucky man, and he became rich by growing tobacco. But many other English colonists and Native Americans living in Virginia were not as lucky.

Tobacco plantations needed a lot of land and a lot of workers. The English colonists were greedy for all the land they could get. This caused several wars to break out between the Native Americans and the English.

By 1625, the colonists had finally won. Although the Native Americans outnumbered the English, the English had guns. This gave them a great advantage. Many Native Americans also died from diseases that had been brought to North America by the colonists.

A Changing Workforce

As time passed, plantations grew larger and larger. Some plantations looked like tiny towns. There was a large house for the owner and small cabins for the field workers. There were other buildings where carpenters and blacksmiths worked.

> **Vocabulary**
>
> **indentured servant,** n. a person who owes an employer a certain amount of work for a certain amount of time in exchange for some benefit

In the early days of the Virginia colony, planters hired **indentured servants** to work in their fields. The plantation owners paid for the indentured servants to sail from England and gave them shelter, food, water, and clothes when they arrived. In exchange, the indentured servants worked for the plantation owners to pay back the money they owed. After a certain number of years, the indentured servants were free to leave. Over time indentured servants came from other countries. Eventually, indentured servants in Virginia were replaced by enslaved workers from Africa.

You will read more about the hard lives of enslaved people in later chapters.

Chapter 6
The Story of Maryland

A Friend of the King In the early 1600s, George Calvert worked for the king of England as a government **official**. The job was very important. Calvert worked hard and did his work well. As a result, the king promised him a reward.

The Big Question

Why was Maryland created, and how did people there escape some of the problems faced by the colonists in Virginia?

Vocabulary

official, n. a person who carries out a government duty

Roman Catholic, n. a person who follows the teachings of the Catholic Church, a Christian church that has its headquarters in Rome, Italy

Protestant, n. a person who follows the teachings of a Christian church that separated from the Roman Catholic Church

The king told Calvert he would give him a lot of land in America. But there was one big problem. George Calvert was a **Roman Catholic**. That made a lot of **Protestant** people very unhappy. They did not want a Catholic to be a government official. Calvert was forced to give up his job.

Almost everybody in England was a Christian. But English Christians were divided into different groups that disliked each other. One group was the Catholics.

The king rewarded George Calvert's service by giving Calvert land in America.

Catholics believed that the **pope** in Rome was the head of the whole Church. Another group was the Protestants. Most English Protestants believed that the king was the head of the Church in England.

Although George Calvert had changed his religion from Protestant to Roman Catholic, the king liked him. He gave Calvert the title of Lord Baltimore—the first Baron of Baltimore. He was named Lord Baltimore after a small place in Ireland. Most people who lived there were Catholics.

Because most of the people in England were Protestants, the laws of England were sometimes unfair to Catholics. But in countries where most of the people were Catholics, such as France, Spain, and Portugal, the laws were sometimes unfair to Protestants.

Maryland's First Owner

George Calvert wanted to start a colony where English Catholics and Protestants would all be treated fairly. This colony would be a refuge, or a place where English Catholics would be protected. The king thought this was a fine idea. So, he gave Calvert permission to build a colony just north of Virginia. The new colony was named Maryland for Queen Henrietta Maria, the king's wife.

George Calvert died shortly after the king gave him Maryland. His oldest son, Cecilius, became the second Lord Baltimore and the new "owner" of Maryland.

Maryland's Second Owner

Unlike Virginia, which was owned by a company, Maryland was owned by one man. Although he lived in England, Cecilius Calvert owned all the land and made all the rules.

The new Lord Baltimore asked his younger brother Leonard to go to Maryland with the first group of colonists. Leonard would be the governor of the new colony. The Calverts started Maryland as a colony for Catholics. But they also wanted Protestants to settle there to increase the colony's population.

The New Colony

In early spring 1634, two small ships sailed into the Chesapeake Bay. Governor Leonard Calvert and nearly two hundred colonists were on board. The ships had no extra space. The passengers had brought with them most of what they would need to survive their first year in the new colony.

Governor Calvert told a group of Native Americans that he wanted to buy one of their villages. The Native Americans were not using the village. They agreed to let the newcomers live there while the colonists built their own houses and planted crops. The governor knew how badly the people in Virginia had suffered. He made sure that the people of his colony had enough food and supplies to avoid a starving time.

Governor Calvert named the colonists' new home Saint Mary's City. This became the first settlement in the Maryland colony.

Home in a Wigwam Village

Two years later, in 1636, the settlement still looked like a Native American village. The colonists lived in wigwams that the Native Americans had built.

Some of the Maryland colonists were wealthy Catholics. But more Protestants than Catholics came to Maryland. Many of the Protestants worked for the Catholic gentlemen as servants.

The colonists had continued to live in traditional Native American wigwams.

Everyone in Saint Mary's City worked hard to get the colony started. Catholic gentlemen and Protestant servants worked side by side. Governor Calvert had the colonists build a chapel, or small church, for Saint Mary's City. Both Catholics and Protestants shared the chapel so that each group could worship in its own way.

In 1649, the **Toleration** Act was created in Maryland. The act gave religious freedom to all Christians in the colony.

> **Vocabulary**
>
> **toleration,** n. acceptance of different beliefs or practices

Tough Times for All

In both Maryland and Virginia, things did not work out as the colonists had hoped. The Virginia Company lost so much money that the king of England took direct control of Virginia.

Many of the first colonists became sick and died.

The Calvert family still owned Maryland, but not too many Catholics actually settled there.

In the early days in Virginia and Maryland, many colonists became sick and died. Children often saw one or both of their parents die. Many children died, too.

At first, Virginia and Maryland planters thought that raising tobacco was almost as good as finding gold. But soon they were shipping so much to England, they could not sell it all. There was too much tobacco and not enough customers. This caused the price of tobacco to drop. After the first few years, anyone who raised tobacco had a very hard time making money.

The only way planters could make money from raising tobacco was to own *lots* of land, have *lots* of workers, and ship *lots* of tobacco to many places. Getting enough land was not that hard to do. Finding workers, however, was more difficult.

Fewer English people were willing to move to Virginia and Maryland to be indentured servants. Keeping indentured servants was also very expensive. Planters needed another way to find large numbers of workers. They found these workers in Africa.

Enslaved people were brought from Africa to grow tobacco in North America.

Servants and Enslaved Workers

The very first Africans were brought to Virginia in the year 1619. Some historians think that these African workers were indentured servants; others believe they may have been enslaved. They worked for a period of time on a plantation, and then they were free to leave. Some became free landowners, just as English indentured servants did.

In the mid-1600s, however, Virginia and Maryland planters changed the rules. Africans brought to the colonies were forced to become enslaved workers. They were considered the property of an owner. They were not paid, and most would never be freed. Their children would become enslaved workers, too. And relying on enslaved workers meant that plantation owners could make more money.

By the late 1600s, large numbers of enslaved Africans were brought to work on plantations near the Chesapeake Bay. They were treated harshly.

In one Southern colony, so many enslaved Africans were brought in that more than half of the people living there were originally from Africa. That colony was called Carolina.

Chapter 7
Plantations in South Carolina

A Charleston Sea Captain It is the year 1710. Eliza and her father are having breakfast at home. Her father, Edward Jones, is a sea captain. Their house overlooks Charleston harbor in the Carolina colony.

The Big Question

Why did plantation owners have enslaved workers?

Captain Jones leaves tomorrow on a long sea voyage. His ships will sail to the West Indies, England, and Africa before returning to Charleston. While her father is at sea, Eliza will live with her uncle, Joseph Jones. He owns two plantations and a house in Charleston.

The port of Charleston lies near the mouths of the Ashley and Cooper rivers. These two rivers connect Charleston to the large plantations inland. From Charleston's harbor, ships can trade with the whole world.

Settling Charleston

In 1710, when Eliza's story takes place, Charleston was the only large town in Carolina colony. In 1663, about thirty years after the Maryland colony began, King Charles II of England gave a group of rich English

Captain Jones will sail to the West Indies, England, Africa, and then back to Charleston. He will take lumber and cattle to the West Indies. In England, he will unload cargo and load other goods. In Africa, he will take on enslaved African workers.

gentlemen another colony in North America. In honor of King Charles, the gentlemen named the colony Carolina. Carolina comes from *Carolus*, which is Latin for Charles.

Wealthy gentlemen started plantations in Carolina to make money by growing cash crops. Tobacco would not grow in the area around Charleston. But Carolina planters discovered they could grow and sell other crops for lots of money. These crops were rice and indigo, a plant from which a blue-green dye is made. A woman by the name of Eliza Lucas was mainly responsible for making indigo a very successful cash crop. Selling these cash crops made some Carolina planters very rich. Like plantation owners in Virginia and Maryland, they began to use enslaved workers.

At the Dock

After breakfast, Eliza and her father go to the dock. Captain Jones looks over his two ships.

The first ship, the *Sea Hawk*, will soon sail for the West Indies. It is filled with lumber and cattle for plantations there.

The second ship, the *Raven*, will sail for England. It will carry a cargo of tobacco, indigo, and rice. In England, the captain will deliver the ship's cargo and buy English goods. The *Raven* will then sail to Africa. There, Captain Edward will trade English goods for enslaved workers. Finally, the *Raven* will sail back to Charleston.

Eliza watches as the sailors load cattle and lumber onto the *Sea Hawk*. On the *Raven*, workers roll huge barrels of rice up the loading ramp and onto the deck.

Trade was an important part of the developing economy in the South.

When the *Raven* reaches Africa, the ship will take enslaved Africans on board. The trip across the Atlantic Ocean, called the **Middle Passage**, is brutal. The enslaved Africans must stay in cramped, dirty quarters beneath the deck of the ship. When the *Raven* returns to Charleston, the enslaved Africans will be sold mostly to plantation owners.

Vocabulary

Middle Passage, n. the forced voyage made by enslaved Africans from Africa to the American colonies

Enslaved Africans were transported from Africa to North America. They were packed onto ships that sailed thousands of miles across the ocean.

Uncle Joseph's Rice Plantation

After a while, a large black carriage pulled by four horses rolls up to the dock. Uncle Joseph and his children appear. Eliza is happy to see her cousins. They travel to Uncle Joseph's new rice plantation. Uncle Joseph is having the plantation built along the banks of the Cooper River, about twenty miles from Charleston.

Much of the land in the new plantation is a **tidal marsh**. The land is a perfect place to grow rice. That is because rice needs a lot of water. But it is not a healthy place to live.

> ### Vocabulary
> **tidal marsh,** n. an area of soft wet land where water levels are the result of the rise and fall of a river or ocean

Many people at the plantation get sick and die. Even those who do not get sick are constantly swatting mosquitoes. They do not know that the mosquitoes spread a deadly disease called malaria.

The long, hot, humid summer months at the plantation are the worst. So, every summer Uncle Joseph's family lives in Charleston. It is a little cooler in Charleston because of breezes from the harbor. People also think they are safer there from disease.

Working in the Fields

Uncle Joseph owns many enslaved workers who had once been rice farmers in Africa. The enslaved workers are digging ditches that will bring water to the rice plants. They have to be careful, for there are many poisonous snakes hiding in the marsh. The enslaved workers are also working in the fields.

The carriage nears the center of the plantation. Eliza sees more enslaved people hard at work. They are building a long driveway leading to the main house.

Many buildings stand behind the trees that line the driveway. Eliza recognizes the sounds coming from the blacksmith's workshop and the horse stable near the carriage house.

A short distance away, soap and candle makers and shoemakers are busy at work. Eliza can see carpenters, gardeners, and stable boys. It takes the hard work of many people to keep the plantation running.

Plantations depended on the hard labor of enslaved workers.

Chapter 8
The Story of Georgia

The Voyage to Savannah The year was 1732, and the ship was called the *Anne*. It was a very crowded ship with 120 passengers and many animals. Most of the people on the *Anne* were poor and unable to find work in England.

The Big Question

Why did James Oglethorpe want to set up a colony in North America?

There was, however, one very wealthy gentleman on the ship. His name was James Oglethorpe (/oh*guhl*thorp/). Everyone called him Father Oglethorpe because he was kind and gentle. James Oglethorpe was the leader of the new colony named Georgia in honor of King George II. It was the last of the Southern Colonies to be established. James Oglethorpe was born into a wealthy family. When he was a teenager, he joined the English army. He became captain of the queen's guard. He left the army when he was twenty-six to become a member of **Parliament**. He spoke out for poor people and for people jailed because they could not pay their **debts**.

Vocabulary

Parliament, n. a group made up of representatives and the king or queen, who make the laws for a country; a term used especially in England to describe the lawmaking part of the government

debt, n. something that is owed, such as money

In England, people often went to jail for a long time if they could not pay their debts. Sometimes they were there until they died.

The Story of Georgia

At the time, people in England who did not have enough money to pay their debts were put into jail. James Oglethorpe wanted to find a way to give debtors and all poor people a new start. He and a group of businessmen asked the king to let them start a colony in North America. They asked him to make the colony a place for poor people to begin a new life.

James Oglethorpe dreamed of building a great city for the Georgia colony. He brought in a city planner to design the new city of Savannah. The streets were wide and straight, and there were many parks.

James Oglethorpe respected Native Americans.

Oglethorpe had many other dreams for the colony. He dreamed of making the Georgia colony a refuge for poor people and for people of different religions from all parts of Europe. He also wanted to keep the colony free of slavery. He had been to Charleston, where he saw how badly enslaved workers were treated.

Oglethorpe also believed Native Americans should be treated fairly and with respect. He made a rule that "no white man may cheat the Native Americans." The Native Americans called James Oglethorpe the "Great Man." They called him that to show their respect for him.

What Happened Next?

Some of Oglethorpe's dreams did not come true. Parliament made it hard for poor people who owed money to leave English jails and settle in Georgia. Rice turned out to be the only crop that could be grown in Georgia and sold for a **profit**. And to grow rice, many workers were needed.

In 1750, the leaders of Georgia decided to change the rules. Slavery and big rice plantations were now allowed, just as in the Carolina colony.

> **Vocabulary**
>
> **profit,** n. the money that is made by a business once all expenses have been paid

Chapter 9
The Pilgrims Come to America

The New England Colonies Do you remember the names of those three regions? If you said Southern Colonies, Middle Colonies, and New England Colonies, you are correct!

The Big Question

Who were the Pilgrims, and why did they sail to America?

Now, we are going to jump over the Middle Colonies and go north to the New England Colonies. We will come back to the Middle Colonies later.

To learn about these colonies, we have to travel back to the fall of 1620 to meet the first New England colonists—the Pilgrims. The Pilgrims spent a great deal of time planning their move to America. At last, in September 1620, they were ready to make the voyage.

The Pilgrims thought long and hard about making the dangerous voyage to North America.

The Pilgrims

"Land ho! Land ho!" the sailors cried. The passengers crowded onto the deck of the *Mayflower*. They wanted to have their first look at America. The *Mayflower* had been sailing for Virginia, but it ended up in what is now Massachusetts.

A month later, the *Mayflower* crossed the bay. On a cold morning in November 1620, its passengers got ready to land. Who were these people on board the ship? Today, we call the *Mayflower*'s passengers the Pilgrims. A pilgrim is someone who travels for religious reasons. The people on the *Mayflower* had left their homes in England for a new life.

The Pilgrims were not like the first Jamestown settlers. The first Jamestown settlers had wanted to find gold and other riches. Many refused to do hard work. They did not want to build houses or plant crops. They only wanted to return to England as rich men.

The Pilgrims were not looking for gold. They wanted to build houses and start farms. They wanted to raise families in a new land. They did not want to go back to England.

In England, King James made everyone obey the rules of the Church of England. The Pilgrims, however, did not wish to do so. They believed so strongly that God wanted them to worship in a certain way that they left the Church of England. They were called Separatists because they wanted to separate, or break away, from the Church of England. That was against the law, and they risked being put in prison.

Trouble for the Separatists

When the king found out about the Separatists, he was angry. He did everything he could to make their lives miserable. He even put some of them in prison.

The Separatists were afraid to stay in England, so they went to the Netherlands. But life there was difficult. People had to work very hard for little money.

The people in the Netherlands spoke Dutch. The Separatists were afraid their children would forget how to speak English.

About twelve years later, the Separatists decided to leave the Netherlands. They wanted to cross the ocean and start a colony. In their new home, they would have their own land and could worship God in their own way.

The *Mayflower* was meant to carry goods, not people.

Not all of the people on the *Mayflower* were Separatists. Other people from England had joined them. Like the Separatists, these people were sailing to America to begin a new life.

A Long, Hard Journey

Altogether, 102 passengers and 30 sailors sailed on the *Mayflower*. There were also some hens, goats, and two dogs.

The journey to North America was difficult. The *Mayflower* was a **cargo ship**. It was not made to carry people. It was very crowded. The Pilgrims slept on the floor below the main deck. There was hardly any light and no fresh air.

> **Vocabulary**
>
> **cargo ship,** n. a large boat used to carry things from one place to another to be bought and sold

For the first month, the *Mayflower* sailed in good weather. After that, the ship and its passengers faced one storm after another. The wind howled and waves crashed on the deck. Most of the passengers became seasick. The Pilgrims were afraid that the ship would sink. The Pilgrims thought the terrible voyage would never end. But finally it did.

Standing on the ship's deck that November morning, the Pilgrims saw a sandy beach lined with trees. This was Cape Cod, Massachusetts. Behind them was the cold, gray, late autumn ocean.

The New Decision

The Pilgrims were excited and afraid. They were very far from home. They were afraid that there might be wild animals.

The Pilgrim leaders said they would have to live on the *Mayflower* until they found a good place to settle and build houses.

Some of the passengers did not like this decision. They were tired of being crowded together on the damp, smelly ship. They wanted to go ashore.

However, the Pilgrim leaders knew that they would have to stay together for safety. If they did not, they would not survive in this new land.

The Pilgrims also knew that they needed rules and laws and good leaders to help them live together peacefully. Before the Pilgrims got off the ship, they wrote and signed a **contract**.

By signing the Mayflower Compact, the Pilgrims were agreeing to work together in the new land.

The Pilgrim leaders called their contract the
Mayflower Compact. The compact said that
all the passengers would work together to
govern themselves in the new land.

The Pilgrims agreed to **vote**. They also
agreed to majority rule. That means the
Pilgrims agreed to do whatever the majority, or most, of the
Pilgrims voted to do. They all promised to obey these rules after
they left the ship.

Starting a New Life

After they signed the Mayflower Compact, the passengers were
allowed to go ashore on Cape Cod. Everyone's legs were wobbly
after being at sea for so long. Even though it had already snowed,
the children ran on the cold, sandy beach. The men searched for
fresh water and dry firewood. They also explored the area.

The women washed clothes. Soon the rocks and bushes were
dotted with clothing spread out to dry.

It took the Pilgrims almost a month to find a permanent place
to settle. They finally decided on a spot on the other side of
Massachusetts Bay from Cape Cod. There the water was deep
enough to anchor their ship.

When they explored the land, they found Native American fields
that had already been cleared for planting. They found freshwater
streams and forests for timber. The Pilgrims named their new
settlement Plymouth.

The Pilgrims were ready to begin a new life.

Chapter 10
Plymouth: The Pilgrim Colony

A Harsh Winter The Pilgrims had hoped to settle in Virginia, but the captain of the *Mayflower* had refused to go farther than Cape Cod. The cold, snowy days of winter had already begun.

The Big Question

Why was it important for the Pilgrims to work hard to prepare for winter?

The Pilgrims spent most of their first winter in Plymouth colony aboard the crowded, damp *Mayflower*. The men and boys went ashore to build the first houses.

An icy wind blew off the ocean. On many days the weather was so bad that the men could not work. During that first winter, half the Pilgrims died from cold and hunger.

All winter, the Native Americans who lived near Plymouth stayed in the forest and watched the Pilgrims. They watched the Pilgrims bring supplies from the ship. They watched them chop down trees and saw logs into planks to build houses.

Despite the cold, wintry conditions, the men and boys set to work building houses.

Setting up a Colony

The first house the Pilgrims built was called the **common house**. At first, it was used as a shelter and a place to store tools. Later, it was used as a place of worship.

When spring finally came, the Pilgrims moved off the *Mayflower* and into the houses. They began to plant crops. They had to work hard. Once the *Mayflower* sailed back to England, they were on their own.

During the warm summer, the Pilgrims tended their gardens. They were already preparing for the winter ahead.

A Visitor

One day a tall Native American warrior with long black hair appeared at the edge of the woods. He walked boldly into Plymouth. The Pilgrims came out of their houses and in from the fields to see the visitor.

"Welcome, Englishmen," he said. "My name is Samoset." The Pilgrims were astonished that he spoke English. It turned out that Samoset had learned the Pilgrims' language from English fishermen who dried their nets and packed their fish along the shore.

Samoset spoke to John Carver, the first governor of Plymouth. He told the governor that the chief of the Wampanoag (/wham*puh*noh*ag/) was coming to visit the Pilgrims. The Wampanoag lived nearby.

Samoset told the Pilgrims about the Native Americans who used to live in the place where the Pilgrims had built their village. These Native Americans had cleared the fields around Plymouth.

A few years before, Samoset told the Pilgrims, a strange sickness had killed every member of that nation.

The only person left in that nation was Squanto, a warrior. Squanto had been taken to England by fishermen before the strange sickness broke out. When Squanto returned, he was the only one of his people still alive.

A Friendship Grows

A few days later, Samoset brought the chief of the Wampanoag to Plymouth colony. With him were several warriors, including Squanto. The Pilgrims and the Native Americans exchanged gifts. Then they ate and drank together. Afterward, Governor Carver and the chief made a peace treaty that lasted fifty-four years.

The chief and the other Native Americans left. But Squanto stayed behind to live with the Pilgrims. He showed the Pilgrims where to fish. He pointed out which nuts and berries were safe to eat.

Squanto taught the Pilgrims how to plant corn and how to trade with other Native Americans.

Boys and girls worked very hard in Plymouth. Everyone had to help prepare for winter.

The Pilgrims were very busy that first spring. Both boys and girls gathered mussels from the rocks in the shallow water at the edge of the sea. They dug clams from the wet sand. They carried water and wood. They stuffed linen sacks with cornhusks to make mattresses.

In the late spring, Governor Carver died. The Pilgrims chose William Bradford as their new governor. Bradford was governor of Plymouth for the next thirty-five years. He even wrote a history of the colony that people today still study.

Giving Thanks

In the fall, Governor Bradford gathered all the Pilgrims together. He told them that they had many things to be thankful for. They had finally found a place to worship God in their own way. And thanks to their Native American friends, their **harvest** would be plentiful. If they were careful, no one would go hungry during the next winter.

Vocabulary

harvest, n. the crops collected at the end of a growing season

To celebrate, Governor Bradford invited the Pilgrims' Native American friends to feast with them and offer prayers of thanksgiving.

The feast lasted three days. That feast was a thanksgiving celebration that has become an American tradition. We do not know for certain whether they ate turkey, but Governor Bradford did write that they had "fowl," or birds, for dinner, as well as other kinds of meat.

When we celebrate Thanksgiving today, we remember how the Pilgrims came to the Americas in search of religious freedom, how much they had to suffer, and how grateful they were for their new life. We also think about the Native Americans who helped them and who shared in their celebration.

The Pilgrims and Native American friends gathered to celebrate the colony's first year.

Chapter 11
The Massachusetts Bay Colony

The Puritan Mission Ten years after the Pilgrims settled Plymouth, more English settlers arrived in New England. Their settlement was called the Massachusetts Bay Colony. These settlers were known as Puritans.

The Big Question

What kinds of jobs were available in the New England colonies?

The Puritans were not like the Pilgrims. The Puritans did not want to leave the Church of England. Instead, the Puritans wanted to purify, or change, the Church of England.

John Winthrop was the leader of the Puritans. He believed that God brought the Puritans to North America for a reason. Winthrop wanted the Puritans to be an example of how Christians could live together in a community and be unselfish people. He believed that the whole world would be watching to see if the Puritans could succeed.

John Winthrop had a plan for the Puritans who traveled to America.

The Great Migration

In the beginning, about one hundred Pilgrims started Plymouth colony. But almost twenty-five thousand Puritans came to Massachusetts Bay Colony from 1630 to 1660. This enormous wave of settlement is called "the Great Migration." A migration is a movement from one place to another.

During the Great Migration, Puritans started small towns all over eastern Massachusetts. In each town, they built their houses and their meetinghouse, or house of worship, near a large grassy area called a common.

Life in Puritan towns centered around the town meetinghouse. Generally, most people lived close to this house of worship.

Strict Rules

Everyone who lived in a Puritan town had to obey strict rules.

Each town was governed by landowning men who met to make rules and decisions. Only members of a town's Puritan **congregation** could own land or vote in the town meeting. Joining a congregation was not easy. You had to answer many hard questions about your life and your beliefs.

70

> **Vocabulary**
>
> **congregation,** n. a group of people who gather for the purpose of religious worship

People who were not Puritans did not enjoy religious freedom. They could attend their own churches. But they were forced to also attend Puritan services and pay taxes to support the Puritan ministers. Those who opposed Puritan religious teachings were punished. Some were forced to leave town. People who were forced to leave Puritan towns sometimes started their own towns. Many of these towns were founded in a new colony called Rhode Island, which you will read about in a later chapter.

A Growing Population

Through the 1640s, new settlers kept coming to the colonies from England. The population was also growing naturally. Unlike in England, and even in the Southern Colonies, more and more New England children lived to become adults and parents. This was largely because there was less disease.

Population Growth in the New England Colonies						
Colony	1650	1660	1670	1680	1690	1700
Connecticut	4,139	7,980	12,603	17,246	21,645	25,970
Massachusetts (including Plymouth)	15,603	22,062	35,333	46,152	56,928	55,941
New Hampshire	1,305	1,555	1,805	2,047	4,164	4,958
Rhode Island	785	1,539	2,155	3,017	4,224	5,894

The population of the New England Colonies grew quickly.

These growing families needed more land. So, two new colonies were later founded by Puritans from Massachusetts. These colonies were Connecticut and New Hampshire.

The New England Region

Although New England was a healthier place to live than the South during the 1600s, the colonies in New England did not have good soil. The winters were long and cold. This meant that the growing season was short. Most New England families could grow only enough food to feed themselves.

However, the region was rich in other ways. There were great forests and a long coastline with natural harbors for ships.

The New England colonists built some of their towns along the coast. These towns became centers for fishing, shipbuilding, and trade.

New Englanders became very good at fishing in the ocean off the coast. This part of the ocean had plenty of fish, especially cod. Cod was tasty, and many people in Europe liked to eat it.

The colonists dried the cod so the meat would not spoil. Then they shipped the cod to England and to the West Indies. Dried cod became to New England what cash crops were to the Southern Colonies.

New Englanders cut timber from the forests for shipbuilding. Tall trees were chopped down to make **masts** for ships. Carpenters cut and shaped the wood to make other parts of the ships. Sailmakers made the ships'

Making barrels was an important skill.

sails, while blacksmiths made the ships' anchors. Men called coopers made barrels to hold cargo, food, and fresh water for long voyages.

Harbor Towns

New England harbor towns were busy places. Ships were loaded with dried cod, timber, and furs. The ships sailed to England, the West Indies, or other colonies.

Other ships arrived with sugar and enslaved workers. Still, more ships brought tools, glassware, and mail from England.

The harbor towns grew faster than the other New England towns. Ships filled with people and their belongings also sailed into the harbor towns. New colonists came to live and work in New England. Fishing and shipbuilding provided jobs for many people. Others found work on the docks and in warehouses.

Chapter 12
Living in a Puritan Colony

Family Life Families were very important to the Puritans. Puritan parents raised their children according to strict rules.

The Big Question

What was life like for children in a Puritan colony?

A School Day

It is the year 1640. In Salem, one of the harbor towns in Massachusetts colony, Patience and Hope have just arrived at Mistress Darby's "dame school." A dame school is a private school run by a woman teacher.

The school is not in a special building like the ones students attend today. It is in Mistress Darby's own small house. And she is *very* strict.

Mistress Darby teaches children in her home.

Parents pay Mistress Darby to teach their children in her kitchen—one of just two rooms in her house. There, Patience and Hope are learning how to read, write, and do arithmetic.

The two girls will attend the dame school together for two years. After that they will stay home and learn how to cook, weave, and sew. They will not go to school anymore. Puritan boys, however, will get the chance to continue their education.

Reading and Writing Lessons

The children have spent the morning practicing their *ABCs* using a hornbook. A hornbook is not really a book. It is a flat board that looks like a paddle. The alphabet is printed on one side. On the other side is a prayer.

In the afternoon, the children are beginning to study their only textbook, the *New England Primer*. It has rhymes that teach the alphabet and spelling words. The *Primer* also has many prayers, poems, and questions about the Bible. Mistress Darby has told each child to learn certain poems by heart. She expects them to be said perfectly.

"Patience!" Mistress Darby calls sharply. "Repeat your lesson."

Patience stands and recites, "Be you to others kind and true, as you'd have others be to you: And neither do nor say to men, whate'er you would not take again."

Patience slowly lets out her breath. She has remembered it correctly.

Mistress Darby seems satisfied—for now!

In **A**dams's Fall
We sinned all.
Thy life to men,
This **B**ook [the Bible]
attend [pay attention to].
The **C**at doth play
And after slay.

A **D**og will bite
A Thief at Night
An **E**agle's flight
Is out of sight.
The idle **F**ool
Is whipped at School.

Rhymes like these helped children learn their *ABCs*.

Finally, it is time to go home. Patience is glad that she remembered her lesson today!

Passing the Meetinghouse

After school, Patience and Hope walk home, crossing the large, grassy common. The common is an open pasture that belongs to everyone in the town. The townspeople bring their cows to graze on the common. The children walk past the meetinghouse. On Sundays, every family in Salem must worship there.

They listen to long **sermons**, read from the Bible, and sing hymns. The service lasts all day, and the **minister** is very serious. His sermons are full of hard words, but Father later explains what the minister has said.

> **Vocabulary**
>
> **sermon,** n. a speech on a religious topic given by a religious leader
>
> **minister,** n. a religious leader, usually in a Protestant church

On Sundays, Patience and Hope know good Puritans are not supposed to do anything except go to the meetinghouse to worship God. They do not even make their beds. Adults do not work, and children certainly are not allowed to play.

Last Sunday, Patience and Hope were both punished. They were running and jumping as the townspeople walked home from the meetinghouse.

A Family Home

Now, coming home from school, Patience and Hope reach the door of their small two-story house. The

The minister is an important member of the community.

downstairs is one large room. It is called the keeping room.

The keeping room is the only room in the house with a fireplace. The fireplace is used for both heating and cooking. It is so big that you can walk right into it and make a small fire in one of the corners! Everyone gathers in the keeping room to eat, to do chores, and to study. In the winter the whole family sleeps here.

The children's father has just come in from the fields with their big brother, Josiah. Their older sister, Honor, is helping their mother prepare a meal. Patience and Hope do not speak. They know that

Puritan fathers expect their children to be silent until he speaks to them first.

An Important Story

Father is telling Josiah how the Puritans came to Massachusetts from England. That was before Patience and Hope were born.

"When we lived in England, we Puritans were not happy with the leaders of the Church of England," Father tells Josiah.

Patience and Hope are quiet. They want to hear the story, too, instead of being sent outside to do chores.

Puritan Beliefs

"The Church of England is too fancy. We do not like its stained-glass windows or the organ music that is played during its worship services. We do not like the fancy robes that its ministers must wear. Many Puritans were thrown in jail because they wanted to change the Church of England. So we decided that we would leave England and come to this new land."

Coming to a New Land

All the children listen carefully as Father continues his story:

"While we were on the ship, Governor Winthrop told us that in Massachusetts we Puritans must be 'as a city upon a Hill.' That means we must be an example for people everywhere in the world to follow.

"We formed a company called the Massachusetts Bay Company. The king gave our company a **charter** to start our own colony in New England. The king was glad to have us move far away from England. He thought we were troublemakers. In 1630, eleven ships, carrying more than seven hundred men, women, and children, sailed to New England."

Working Together

Father continues: "When we arrived, we could see that New England was beautiful. The trees were so green! The forests were full of deer, and the ocean was filled with fish. We worked very hard to settle here."

Father turns to Patience and Hope.

"Children," he says, "you have learned how we Puritans came to New England. But it is time to go back to work. You both have chores to do outside, and I have wood to chop."

The girls smile at their father before racing outside to the garden.

Just like all Puritan children, Patience and Hope had chores to do.

Chapter 13
The Story of Rhode Island

An English Man Roger Williams was born in London, England. As a boy, he learned to write in a special way called **shorthand**. When he went to church, he used shorthand to write down what the minister said. Roger's shorthand notes helped him to study the Bible.

The Big Question

What was the main reason why Roger Williams disagreed with his fellow Puritans?

When Roger grew up, he went to Cambridge University, one of England's famous schools. During his time at Cambridge, he became a Puritan, and eventually he became a minister.

Vocabulary

shorthand, n. a system of abbreviations and symbols used to make writing faster

household, n. a house and all of the people who live within it

Wanting Freedom

Roger Williams knew that the king did not like Puritans because they disagreed with the Church of England. Roger Williams worked as a minister in the **household** of a Puritan who was a member of Parliament. There, he met Puritans who wanted to leave England and live in North America.

As a young boy, Roger spent a lot of time studying.

Roger Williams decided to join the Puritans in Massachusetts. He wanted to be free of the king and the church leaders in England.

However, as you have discovered, the Puritans who traveled to Massachusetts were not Separatists like the Pilgrims in Plymouth. Puritans wanted to change the Church of England by example.

In 1631, Roger Williams sailed to Boston, Massachusetts. Governor John Winthrop offered him a job as minister to Boston's Puritan congregation. Roger Williams now disagreed with his fellow Puritans. He believed that it was time to leave the Church of England. Williams told Governor Winthrop that he could not take the job.

Expressing His Beliefs

Roger Williams found other work as a minister, first in Plymouth and then in Salem. He spoke out against forcing people to pay taxes to support Puritan congregations. He feared that close ties with the government were harming the Church. He also thought that Puritans were not strict enough in their religious beliefs. Puritan leaders became angry with Roger Williams.

Roger Williams also believed that the king had no right to take land from Native Americans. Williams said the colonists should pay the Native Americans for any land they wished to have. Williams became friends with a group of Native Americans. He knew many languages, including Latin, Greek, and Hebrew, and he learned their language, too. Williams earned the respect of the Native Americans.

The Puritans Disagree

The Puritans decided to send Roger Williams back to England. It was almost winter, and he was sick. So, Governor Winthrop said that Williams could wait and return to England in the spring.

But Williams did not wish to return to England. Instead, he escaped from Massachusetts and went to what is now Rhode Island. There, he spent the winter with his Native American friends, the Wampanoag.

In the spring, some of Williams's Puritan friends came to help him. He built a house and planted crops.

Williams bought land from the Narragansett Native Americans. With his Puritan friends, Roger Williams started a town on that land. He called the town Providence. It was the first town in the colony that would eventually be called Rhode Island.

Before the Puritans could send Roger Williams back to England, he escaped in the middle of the night.

Where the People Rule

The town of Providence was ruled by the people, not by the members of a religious congregation. People had religious freedom. They were not punished for their beliefs, even if Williams disagreed with them.

Unlike in Massachusetts, the people living in Rhode Island were not forced to pay taxes to support the Puritan congregation. In fact, no taxes were paid to any religious group. People of different religions who settled in Providence were responsible for supporting themselves.

Anne Hutchinson

Little by little, more towns were set up near Providence. Like Roger Williams, another famous Puritan moved from Massachusetts to Rhode Island. She was a very brave woman named Anne Hutchinson.

Anne Hutchinson always spoke her mind. She read the Bible very carefully. She believed that God inspired her directly. She said that she did not need the Puritan ministers telling her what to believe. Like Roger Williams, Anne did not believe that the Puritans were strict enough in their beliefs. The Puritans did not like having people challenge their religious beliefs, especially a woman.

Like Roger Williams, Anne Hutchinson soon got into trouble with Governor Winthrop and the other Puritan leaders. When the Puritan leaders ordered her and her family to leave Massachusetts, her friends helped her start the new town of Portsmouth, Rhode Island.

Puritan leaders did not like that Anne Hutchinson disagreed with them.

A Successful Colony

As the number of towns in Rhode Island grew, the people wanted to have their own official colony. Roger Williams traveled to England to ask the king for a charter for the colony. Williams still had friends in Parliament. They helped him get the charter.

People in Rhode Island had more religious freedom than in any other colony. Most of them liked Roger Williams. He was eventually elected president of the colony.

Williams worked for the rest of his life to make Rhode Island a good place to live. He worked to keep peace with Native Americans. He treated everyone with kindness and respect.

Roger Williams's ideas about separating religion from government can still be found in our laws today.

Chapter 14
The Middle Colonies

Different Colonies There are still four colonies to learn about: New York, New Jersey, Delaware, and Pennsylvania. These colonies are called the Middle Colonies. Both the Southern Colonies and New England Colonies attracted colonists mostly from England and Scotland. But people from many different parts of Europe came to the Middle Colonies.

The Big Question

How did the mixing of cultures help the Middle Colonies grow and prosper?

Vocabulary

culture, n. the language, religion, customs, traditions, and material possessions of a group of people

Settlers came from Germany, the Netherlands (also called Holland), and Sweden. Some of these people came for religious freedom. Some came to trade with Native Americans. Others looked for farmland to grow crops. To get along, people in the Middle Colonies had to respect each other's differences. They had to respect the different religions, **cultures**, and languages.

Not all the people who came to the Middle Colonies spoke the same language. They also had different religions and customs.

A Mixing of Cultures

Colonists from different countries brought unique skills to the Middle Colonies. The Germans were skilled farmers. The Dutch were very good at building wagons and **plows**. The Swedes built strong log houses.

> **Vocabulary**
>
> **plow,** n. a tool used to prepare soil for farming

The colonists taught these skills to each other. Sometimes they even shared ways to have fun. For example, the Dutch taught the other colonists about ice skating and bowling.

Sharing among different peoples caused cultures to mix. This mixing of cultures helped the Middle Colonies grow and prosper.

Farming in the Middle Colonies

Like the New England Colonies, the Middle Colonies had large forests. The forests provided lumber for building things like houses and ships.

But unlike New England, the Middle Colonies were a good place to farm. The soil was rich. The climate was usually mild. Summers were warm and rainy. Many kinds of crops grew well there.

The early settlers grew different kinds of fruits and vegetables. Farmers grew enough crops to feed their families. They also had enough left over to sell for a profit.

Soon farmers grew cash crops just to sell. The main cash crops in the Middle Colonies were grains, such as wheat, rye, and oats. Because the Middle Colonies grew large amounts of grains, they were called the "breadbasket colonies."

River Highways

After the harvest, many farmers took their wheat to a miller. The miller, a person who owns a mill, would then grind the wheat into flour.

After the wheat was harvested, it was brought to a mill. Early mills were often powered by water.

Now the farmers were ready to sell their flour in markets in big port cities, such as Philadelphia and New York City. But how would they get the flour there?

Farmers in Pennsylvania used the Delaware River to move crops from their farms to Philadelphia. Farmers in New York used the Hudson River to move crops to markets in New York City. Both the Delaware and Hudson rivers are very wide and deep. This made it possible for ships to travel almost one hundred miles upstream.

When the farmers reached Philadelphia or New York City, they sold their flour and other crops to **merchants**. Sometimes the merchants shipped the crops to other colonies. Other times the merchants shipped the crops to England or other European countries.

> **Vocabulary**
>
> **merchant,** n. a person who buys and sells things to earn money

Important Cities

New York City and Philadelphia became centers for trade and shipping. They also became centers for the mixing of cultures. People with special skills and new ideas came to these port cities. They started schools, built libraries, and printed newspapers.

Over time, different cultures, beliefs, and ideas began to create something entirely new—an American culture.

People from all over brought their ideas and traditions to the Middle Colonies.

Chapter 15
New York: A Dutch Settlement

Dutch Culture The Dutch colonists brought many things to the North American colonies. They brought foods, such as waffles and coleslaw. They brought activities, such as sledding, ice-skating, and bowling. They even brought the idea of Santa Claus.

The Big Question

Why was Peter Stuyvesant unable to defend New Amsterdam against the English?

Their colony was located right in the middle of England's North American colonies. It was between the Puritan towns of New England and the plantations of the Southern Colonies.

An Explorer for the Dutch

It was a pleasant September morning in 1609, about two years after the Jamestown settlers sailed up the James River in Virginia. An explorer sailed his small ship up a wide, deep river. He was looking for a waterway through North America to Asia.

The Dutch colonists brought new foods to North America, such as waffles and coleslaw.

The explorer's name was Henry Hudson. He was an Englishman. But he was working for the Dutch. The river he found is now called the Hudson River.

A Good Trading Post

Henry Hudson did not find a waterway to Asia. Instead he found Native Americans who wanted to trade valuable furs for his tools, weapons, and colorful cloth.

Hudson also found dense forests and good land for farming. He claimed a large area of this land for the Dutch.

The Dutch decided the territory would make a great trading post. They called the trading post New Netherland after their homeland.

In 1621, a group of wealthy Dutchmen formed the Dutch West India Company. The Dutch government gave the Dutch West India Company the right to settle New Netherland and the right to trade with Native Americans. The company named a governor to run the new colony. The colony's purpose was to make the people who owned the company rich.

The company sent a ship to New Netherland with 110 people. The biggest group started a settlement far up the Hudson River in a place that is now Albany, New York. That was as far up the river as oceangoing ships could sail. It was a good place to buy furs from the Native Americans, especially the Haudenosaunee. Furs sold for very high prices in Europe.

A smaller group settled on Manhattan, an island at the mouth of the Hudson River. This small group built a fort on the island.

Buying an Island

The next year more people came to the island of Manhattan. They built a town they called New Amsterdam, after the city of Amsterdam in the Netherlands. The governor of New Netherland, Peter Minuit, thought it was a good idea to buy the whole island from the Native Americans.

The governor offered some cloth, knives, beads, and other small things to the Native Americans in exchange for Manhattan Island. The total value of everything the governor offered was said to be about $24.

The governor probably thought he had done very well in the trade. The Native Americans probably thought they had done very well

The Dutch traded with Native Americans for the island of Manhattan.

too. Native Americans did not think about owning land in the same way as Europeans. They did not think that land could be *owned* by anyone. They believed they were giving the land to the Dutch to use, not to possess.

Settling New Amsterdam

The Dutch built houses, streets, and public buildings in New Amsterdam. The houses they built were tall and narrow with steep roofs. They looked like houses back in the Netherlands.

The Dutch built a wall across the island at one end of the town. Outside the wall, they started farms that they called *bouweries* (/boo*ve*reez/).

The Dutch worked in their new town. They also loved to have fun. Boys and girls in New Amsterdam went to school year-round. The Dutch settlers even had special holidays.

One of their holidays was called First Skating Day. That was the first day that the ponds were frozen hard enough for ice skating. On that day, the schools closed and the whole town went ice skating.

A Tolerant People and a Harsh Leader

Most Dutch people were tolerant. They invited people from other countries to move to New Amsterdam.

Peter Stuyvesant (/sty*vuh*sent/) was named the second governor of New Amsterdam. Stuyvesant had a wooden leg. If he did not get his way, he would stamp his wooden leg and swear.

Stuyvesant disliked anyone who disagreed with him. When someone disagreed with him, he threatened to ship the person back to the Netherlands—in pieces.

New Amsterdam was doing well, but it was growing quite slowly. Most of the Dutch people back in the Netherlands were happy. They did not want to move to America. They had jobs and they had **freedom of religion**. Very few wanted to travel thousands of miles to start over in New Netherland.

The English Take Over

Life was very different for the people who lived in England in the 1600s. They had many good reasons to leave.

The king wanted an English colony, not a Dutch colony, between the New England Colonies and the Southern Colonies. New Amsterdam was valuable because it was the gateway to the Hudson River, a valuable trade route.

In 1664, a war started between England and the Netherlands. The king of England gave his brother the job of taking New Netherland from the Dutch. The king promised his brother, the Duke of York, that he could have the colony if he was successful.

The Duke of York sent warships and several hundred soldiers to New Amsterdam. As the ships sailed into the harbor, the English prepared to fight.

The Duke of York sent several hundred soldiers to capture New Amsterdam for England.

Peter Stuyvesant became very angry. He wanted to fight the English, but he could not. First, he did not have enough gunpowder to fire his cannons. Second, he did not have enough soldiers to defend the town. And finally, almost everyone in New Amsterdam refused to help him. They wanted him to surrender. That way, no one would get hurt.

Peter Stuyvesant had no choice but to surrender. The English took the colony of New Netherland without firing a single shot.

The English and Dutch Get Along

The Dutch and the English got along well in the New York colony. The people continued to work hard, but they also had fun. The Dutch and the English even shared the church buildings for religious services.

Peter Stuyvesant was forced to surrender New Netherland to the English.

The English allowed freedom of religion just like the Dutch. They even allowed Peter Stuyvesant to stay, but he was not in charge anymore. He became a farmer on Manhattan Island.

New York City

Today, New Amsterdam is called New York City. The place where the Dutch built their wall is still known as Wall Street. That wall was built to keep farm animals from wandering into the town. In the tall buildings along Wall Street today, businesses make deals worth millions—even billions—of dollars every day.

The area where the Dutch had their farms, or *bouweries*, is now called the Bowery. Amsterdam Avenue is a very busy street in New York City. High schools, parks, and even a neighborhood are even named after Peter Stuyvesant.

Chapter 16
William Penn and the Quakers

An Important Letter William Penn sat at his desk in his large house in England. He looked down at the charter in front of him. The king of England had signed the charter. It was dated 1681.

The Big Question

Why might Philadelphia have been a place that Europeans would want to move to?

The charter gave William Penn the right to start a colony in North America. The name of the colony would be Pennsylvania, which means Penn's Woods.

Before he left England, Penn wrote a letter to the Native Americans who lived in his new colony.

First, Penn told the Native Americans that he and his colonists would sail to North America soon. They planned to arrive in the summer of 1682.

Next, Penn told the Native Americans that he knew they had been mistreated by English colonists in the past. He promised that the Pennsylvania colonists would be kind and fair. Any colonist who harmed Native Americans would be punished.

William Penn wanted to treat the Native Americans fairly and with respect.

Penn ended his letter by saying that he had a great love and respect for the Native Americans and he hoped to win their love and friendship.

Quaker Beliefs

William Penn was a Quaker. The Quakers belonged to a religious group called the Society of Friends. The Quakers' way of worship was very different from worship in the Church of England. The Quakers did not have ministers who gave sermons. When the Quakers met in their meetinghouses, they prayed silently. During the meeting, anyone who felt inspired by God could stand up and speak to the others.

The Friends believed that all people were equal and should be treated with respect. They believed that the **aristocracy** was no better than other people. But the aristocracy in England did not agree. They expected everyone to bow to them and call them *my lord* or *my lady*.

> **Vocabulary**
>
> **aristocracy,** n. the upper or noble class whose members' status is usually inherited

Because the Bible says, "Thou shalt not kill," the Quakers believed all wars were wrong. The Quakers would not join armies or fight wars.

Hard Times for the Quakers

The Quakers had many enemies in England. Some thought that the Friends were troublemakers. The government disliked them because they said war was wrong. The Church of England was angry about the Quakers' religious ideas. As a result, many

William Penn, like many other Quakers, was put in prison for his religious beliefs.

Quakers were put in prison for their beliefs. Life in England became harder and harder for the Society of Friends.

William Penn was perhaps the best-known Quaker in England. Because of his Quaker beliefs, Penn had also been sent to jail several times.

Settling Pennsylvania

William Penn was a good person to lead a colony. He was a lawyer and a town planner. He was also a just man who treated all people fairly.

Penn called his colony a "holy experiment." He wanted Pennsylvania to be a place where Quakers and other religious groups could live together in harmony.

Penn also opened his new colony to people who were not Quakers. To advertise his colony, Penn printed booklets. In his booklets, he told about the beauty of the land, and he promised religious freedom for everyone who settled in Pennsylvania.

Planning Philadelphia

Penn helped design the city of Philadelphia, the first major city in Pennsylvania. In Greek, the name *Philadelphia* means "brotherly love." This name was very fitting for the Quaker city.

William Penn's plan for the city looked like a checkerboard. He laid out the streets in that pattern. He gave numbers to all the streets that ran from north to south. Penn gave tree names, like Pine and Walnut, to streets that ran from east to west. He put in a

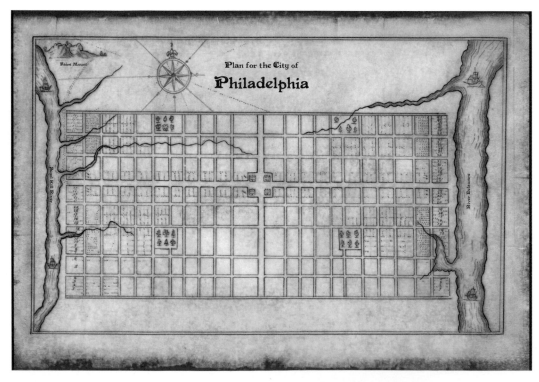

William Penn made a city plan for Philadelphia that included parks and gardens.

central square where people could meet. He planned many parks and gardens.

Penn did not have walls or **stockades** built around Philadelphia. He said it was a city where everyone would live in peace. Soon other colonial towns used Penn's city plan as an example.

Philadelphia grew very quickly. The colonists could not build houses fast enough. Some colonists had to live in caves along the banks of the Delaware River while they built their houses.

William Penn soon returned to England. He spent less than four years of his life in Pennsylvania. He spent most of his time in England, defending the rights of the settlers in Pennsylvania.

Delaware Valley Settlers

People from all over Europe settled in Pennsylvania for many reasons. They came for religious freedom. They came because they could afford to buy the rich farmland, and the climate was mild for farming. They came for the promise of good trade. They also came because the colony was at peace with Native Americans.

Two other Middle Colonies were also located along the Delaware River Valley: New Jersey and Delaware. Before William Penn's colony, Dutch and Swedish settlements existed in this area.

When England took over New Netherland and renamed it New York, the king made New Jersey an English colony, too. At the beginning of the 1700s, some Pennsylvania settlers formed the new colony of Delaware.

Philadelphia

It did not take long for Philadelphia to become an important city in the colonies. Philadelphia was a busy port and trading center.

Land in Pennsylvania, Delaware, and New Jersey was fertile. Farms prospered in all three colonies. Farmers sold their crops in Philadelphia. Ships loaded with flour, grains, and dried fruit sailed to other ports in the colonies. The ships also sailed across the Atlantic Ocean to England and Europe.

Because there was so much trade in Philadelphia, there were many kinds of jobs. People worked as farmers, bakers, blacksmiths, toolmakers, tailors, and glassmakers. People also worked as teachers, printers, booksellers, and lawyers.

Many skilled people worked in Philadelphia.

As Philadelphia grew, the city built paved streets and raised sidewalks with curbs. At night, lamps burned whale oil to light the main streets.

Most people in Philadelphia lived in small brick houses. But in the 1700s, a few wealthy people built big houses. They filled them with beautiful furniture and art.

Because of trade and the mixing of cultures, Philadelphia became a great center for new ideas. As time went on, people in Philadelphia built a college, a theater, and America's first hospital. They also built a museum, a public library, and started a scientific society.

By 1776, when the American colonies rebelled against British rule and declared their **independence**, Philadelphia was the largest city in the thirteen colonies. In fact, it was the second-largest English-speaking city in the whole world after London!

> **Vocabulary**
>
> **independence,** n. freedom from the control of a person or group of people

Glossary

A

aristocracy, n. the upper or noble class whose members' status is usually inherited (104)

C

cargo ship, n. a large boat used to carry things from one place to another to be bought and sold (58)

cash crop, n. a crop that is grown to be sold (31)

charter, n. a document given by a ruler to a group of people that allows them to elect their own government officials (80)

"common house," (phrase) a building used for meetings and worship (64)

congregation, n. a group of people who gather for the purpose of religious worship (70)

contract, n. a written or spoken agreement, usually about business (59)

council, n. group of people who meet to help run a government (13)

crop, n. a plant that is grown in large quantities for food or other use (7)

culture, n. the language, religion, customs, traditions, and material possessions of a group of people (88)

D

debt, n. something that is owed, such as money (50)

deck, n. the floor of a ship that people walk on (14)

disease, n. sickness (34)

F

"freedom of religion," (phrase) the ability to practice any religion without fear of punishment (99)

G

gentleman, n. a man with high position in society; not a laborer (14)

governor, n. a person appointed by the king to oversee and make decisions in a region or colony (26)

gunpowder, n. an explosive material used to make guns shoot (24)

H

harbor, n. a part of a body of water that is next to land and provides a safe place for ships to anchor (7)

harvest, n. the crops collected at the end of a growing season (67)

household, n. a house and all of the people who live within it (82)

I

indentured servant, n. a person who owes an employer a certain amount of work for a certain amount of time in exchange for some benefit (35)

independence, n. freedom from the control of a person or group of people (109)

M

mast, n. a large vertical post on a ship that helps hold up the sails (72)

merchant, n. a person who buys and sells things to earn money (92)

Middle Passage, n. the forced voyage made by enslaved Africans from Africa to the American colonies (47)

minister, n. a religious leader, usually in a Protestant church (77)

O

official, n. a person who carries out a government duty **(36)**

P

palisade, n. a fence made from wooden or metal stakes driven into the ground **(15)**

Parliament, n. a group made up of representatives and the king or queen, who make the laws for a country; a term used especially in England to describe the lawmaking part of the government **(50)**

plow, n. a tool used to prepare soil for farming **(90)**

pope, n. the head of the Roman Catholic Church **(38)**

profit, n. the money that is made by a business once all expenses have been paid **(53)**

Protestant, n. a person who follows the teachings of a Christian church that separated from the Roman Catholic Church **(36)**

R

region, n. a large area that may have certain characteristics related to its geography, form of government, or traditions that set it apart from other places **(6)**

Roman Catholic, n. a person who follows the teachings of the Catholic Church, a Christian church that has its headquarters in Rome, Italy **(36)**

S

self-government, n. the ability of people to rule themselves and make their own laws **(32)**

sermon, n. a speech on a religious topic given by a religious leader **(77)**

shorthand, n. a system of abbreviations and symbols used to make writing faster **(82)**

stockade, n. a defensive wall, usually made from stakes or poles driven into the ground **(107)**

T

tidal marsh, n. an area of soft wet land where water levels are the result of the rise and fall of a river or ocean **(48)**

timber, n. wood that is cut from trees and used for building; lumber **(7)**

tobacco, n. a plant whose leaves are used for chewing or smoking **(31)**

toleration, n. acceptance of different beliefs or practices **(40)**

trader, n. a person who buys and sells things **(2)**

V

vote, v. to make a decision as a group, usually by casting ballots, raising hands, or speaking aloud **(60)**

W

well, n. a hole dug deep into the ground to get water **(20)**

Core Knowledge®

CKHG™
Core Knowledge HISTORY AND GEOGRAPHY™

Series Editor-In-Chief
E.D. Hirsch, Jr.

Editorial Directors
Linda Bevilacqua and Rosie McCormick

Subject Matter Expert

J. Chris Arndt, PhD

Department of History, James Madison University

Tony Williams

Senior Teaching Fellow, Bill of Rights Institute